ENGINEERING CHALLENGES

BUILDING BRIDGES

by Samantha S. Bell

FOCUS READERS

FOCUS READERS

WWW.FOCUSREADERS.COM

Focus Readers is distributed by North Star Editions:
sales@northstareditions.com | 888-417-0195

Produced for Focus Readers by Red Line Editorial.

Content Consultant: Arielle Ehrlich, State Bridge Design Engineer, Minnesota Department of Transportation

Photographs ©: Anastasios71/Shutterstock Images, cover; unge255_stock/Shutterstock Images, 4–5; SeanPavonePhoto/iStockphoto, 7; chrisdorney/iStockphoto, 9; Lyubov Pogorela/Shutterstock Images, 10–11; RoschetzkyIstockPhoto/iStockphoto, 13; Joe Christensen/iStockphoto, 14; cchan/iStockphoto, 17; Wide World/Library of Congress, 18–19; stillhope/iStockphoto, 21; Tagstock1/iStockphoto, 22–23; Red Line Editorial, 24–25, 27, 28

ISBN
978-1-63517-251-5 (hardcover)
978-1-63517-316-1 (paperback)
978-1-63517-446-5 (ebook pdf)
978-1-63517-381-9 (hosted ebook)

Library of Congress Control Number: 2017935927

Printed in the United States of America
Mankato, MN
June, 2017

ABOUT THE AUTHOR

Samantha S. Bell is the author of more than 50 nonfiction books for children. She worked for several years for her father, an architect and engineer who created all kinds of structures. One summer, she helped her family build a truss bridge over a large creek in Tennessee.

TABLE OF CONTENTS

CHAPTER 1

CROSSING AND CONNECTING

Twelve-year-old Jin stands in line with his family. He is waiting for his turn to walk across the Zhangjiajie Grand Canyon glass bridge in China. The bridge is made of 99 glass panels. Each has three layers and can support 40 tons (36 metric tons). Finally, it's Jin's turn to cross the amazing 1,400-foot (430-m) bridge.

Tourists walk across the Zhangjiajie Grand Canyon glass bridge.

Jin watches as some visitors hold the railings. Others crawl on their hands and knees. But Jin walks bravely across. He can see the 1,000-foot (300-m) drop beneath his feet.

Bridges are structures people use to get across a river, road, or other obstacle. Bridges are built in different ways depending on the climate, terrain, and materials available. A bridge can be a simple piece of rope. Or it can be a complex structure of towers and cables.

The ancient Romans were among the first to show their skills in bridge building. Their bridges had arches made of stone. But they needed to make

The Romans built this bridge in Cordoba, Spain, during ancient times.

the bridges stronger and sturdier. By 2 BCE, they had discovered how to make waterproof concrete. Using a **cofferdam**, they could make a concrete bridge.

The ancient Chinese also built bridges. They used wood, stone, bamboo, and iron chain.

Bridge design did not change much until the 1100s. At that time, the Catholic Church saw the importance of good roads for communication. That meant more bridges were needed. Priests worked to design and construct them.

Traders also needed bridges. They traveled from city to city with their goods. As the centuries passed, bridge builders introduced new types of materials. These materials led to new building methods. Bridge construction became more scientific than ever before.

Engineers are still designing, building, and improving bridges today. These structures do more than just

Tower Bridge crosses the River Thames in London, England.

cross an **expanse**. Some help inspire emotions, such as awe or wonder. Others **commemorate** significant events. But they all are a way to connect people with their communities.

CHAPTER 2

STRONG DESIGNS, STRONG BRIDGES

Architects and engineers work to design bridges that are functional, safe, and often beautiful. One of the first things they consider is the dead load. This is the weight of the structure itself. Next, they consider the live load. This is the people and objects that will cross the bridge.

The Bay Bridge crosses San Francisco Bay in California.

Engineers plan for other factors as well. For example, they plan for natural events such as ice, wind, or earthquakes. They also consider what might happen on the bridge, such as vehicles hitting the bridge.

Next, they must choose the best materials to use. The bridge needs to be strong enough to carry all of the loads that will travel on the bridge. But in most cases, the planners have a budget. As a result, the materials cannot be too expensive. Bridges can be built of stone, iron, wood, aluminum, or even plastic. However, many modern bridges are made of steel or concrete.

A bridge must be strong enough to support dead and live loads.

Engineers also consider the forces that will act on the bridge. Tension pulls things apart. Compression pushes things together. If there is too much of either, the material will not be able to carry the loads. That could cause the bridge to fail.

Arches are strong shapes, so engineers often use them when designing bridges.

Different bridge designs handle these forces in different ways.

A beam bridge is one of the simplest designs. These bridges usually have at least two horizontal beams supported by

substructures. The beams carry the loads into the substructures.

Truss bridges are made from a framework of smaller elements. These elements are often built in a triangular pattern. The triangles distribute the stress throughout the structure. They carry the load through tension or compression.

Arch bridges get their strength from their semicircle shape. This shape carries compression from the top of the arch down to the supports in the ground.

Suspension bridges are used for the longest spans. These bridges have high towers with two main cables.

ENGINEERING DESIGN PROCESS

Engineers must be confident in their plans. They use various tools and do many tests in their planning. By following the engineering design process, the bridge should be strong enough for the loads.

ASK: What needs to be crossed? Who or what will be crossing it? What natural factors might affect the bridge? What materials are available?

IMAGINE: Brainstorm possible bridge designs. What type of bridge would work best?

PLAN: Draw a diagram or create a model of the bridge. Make a list of materials needed. Write down the steps that will need to be taken to build it.

CREATE: Follow the plan and build a bridge.

IMPROVE: What worked with the bridge? What could be made better? How could the design change to make the bridge stronger?

This suspension bridge crosses 230 feet (70 m) above the Capilano River in British Columbia.

The cables extend from the land, over the towers, and back to the land on the other side. Smaller cables hang from the main cables and attach to the **deck**. The deck is held up by the cables. **Cable-stayed bridges** are another kind of a suspension bridge.

CHAPTER 3

GALLOPING GERTIE

Sometimes engineers make mistakes. The Tacoma Narrows Bridge was the first to cross the Puget Sound in Washington. But to keep costs down, the designer made the bridge narrower and more flexible than normal. Other engineers noticed that wind caused the bridge's deck to have wave motions.

The Tacoma Narrows Bridge collapsed in 1940.

They tried to take the bounce out by using **hydraulic jacks** as shock absorbers. However, nothing worked. The bridge became known as Galloping Gertie.

Even as Gertie opened in July 1940, engineers were trying to fix it. The next step was to add wind **deflectors**. But the engineers were too late. On November 7, steady winds blew. The deck moved up and down in waves up to 5 feet (1.5 m) high. Then a cable slipped, and Gertie began to twist. The motions became larger and larger. Within minutes, the roadway was tilting up to 28 feet (8.5 m) high. In a little more than an hour, the bridge broke apart and fell into the water.

Galloping Gertie collapsed four months after it opened. Today there are two new bridges in its place.

Fortunately, people who had been on the bridge were safe. A replacement bridge was completed in 1950. It was called Sturdy Gertie. The new design included wind grates and hydraulic shock absorbers. This time, trusses were used to stiffen the bridge. In 2007, a second bridge was added to help with traffic.

THE PEARL BRIDGE

In 1998, the Akashi Kaikyo Bridge in Japan became the world's longest suspension bridge. Its span is nearly 1.24 miles (1.99 km) long. The structure is known as the Pearl Bridge. More than 1,000 lights are attached to its cables. At night, they look like a string of pearls.

Engineers designing the bridge faced natural challenges. The bridge was built in water 360 feet (110 m) deep. The ground under the bridge could experience an earthquake. Meanwhile, winds could reach speeds up to 179 miles per hour (288 km/h). To be sure the design worked, researchers built the world's largest wind tunnel facility to test it. In total, construction of the bridge took 10 years.

The Pearl Bridge was built to survive many natural challenges.

BOOKS IN
BIGGEST NAMES IN SPORTS

Get to know some of today's most popular... Find out
's, amazing feats, and learn about...
'e the scenes. These captivat...
re to be a hit with fans of...

BECKHAM JR.
...US BRYANT
...LL STAR
...BALL STAR
...ETBALL

CHAPTER 4

BUILD A BRIDGE!

Now it is your turn to build a bridge. Yours should hold a live load of several paperclips. It should span across two stacks of books.

Materials:

For this challenge, you'll need paper (different types), books, a ruler, scissors, tape, and paperclips.

Build a bridge that can hold a live load.

Procedure:

1. Place the books in two towers approximately 8 inches (20 cm) apart. Place a sheet of paper on the books so it spans the space between them.

2. Test the bridge by adding one paperclip at a time to the paper. How many paperclips will it hold?

3. Try a new design. Fold one long side of the paper 2 inches (5 cm) in toward the center. Do the same with the other long side of the paper. Open your paper and place it on the books. The paper bridge now has two raised sides.

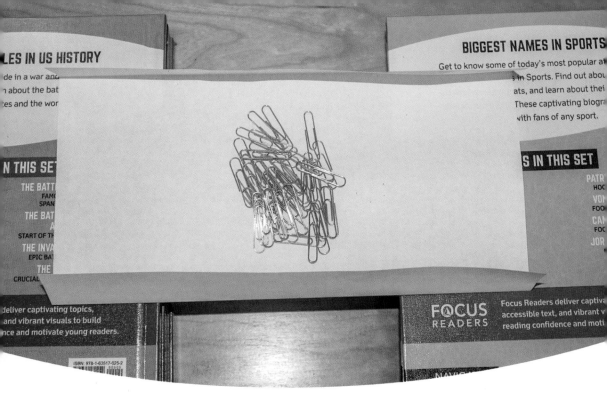

Adding raised sides to your bridge can make it stronger.

4. Test the new bridge by adding one paperclip at a time to the paper. How many paperclips will it hold?

5. Fold a second piece of paper like the first. Stack the two papers on top of each other. How many paperclips does the bridge hold now?

 Different designs and materials can help make your bridge stronger than ever.

6. Next, take a third sheet of paper. Fold it back and forth about five times like a fan. Place this paper on top of the books. Place a new flat sheet of paper on top of it. How many paperclips does the bridge hold now?

Improve It!

- The fan design created triangles that worked like trusses to support more weight. How can you make the bridge even stronger?

- Use some paper and tape to make substructures. Where could you place the substructures to add the most support?

- Try using different kinds of paper, such as notebook paper, construction paper, or cardstock. Which materials work the best?

FOCUS ON
BUILDING BRIDGES

Write your answers on a separate piece of paper.

1. Write a letter to a friend describing what you learned about Galloping Gertie.

2. Many bridges are built to be beautiful as well as functional. Which of the basic bridge designs do you like the best? Why?

3. What does tension do?

   A. pushes materials together
   B. twists materials
   C. pulls materials apart

4. In a beam bridge, what happens when the substructures are placed farther apart on the same beam?

   A. The bridge becomes stronger.
   B. The bridge becomes weaker.
   C. The bridge stays the same.

Answer key on page 32.

GLOSSARY

cable-stayed bridges
Bridges with cables that attach directly from a tower to the deck.

cofferdam
A temporary, watertight space used to build the foundations of a bridge.

commemorate
To use as a memorial or remembrance.

deck
The surface of a bridge used by people, animals, or vehicles.

deflectors
Devices that cause something to turn or change direction.

expanse
A wide area or space.

hydraulic jacks
Devices that use a small amount of force to lift a heavy load.

substructures
The parts of a bridge that support the span from underneath.

TO LEARN MORE

BOOKS

Graham, Ian. *Fabulous Bridges.* Mankato, MN: Amicus, 2011.

Hayes, Amy. *Building Bridges and Roads: Civil Engineers.* New York: PowderKids Press, 2016.

Latham, Donna. *Bridges and Tunnels: Investigate Feats of Engineering with 25 Projects.* White River Junction, VT: Nomad Press, 2012.

NOTE TO EDUCATORS

Visit **www.focusreaders.com** to find lesson plans, activities, links, and other resources related to this title.

INDEX

Answer Key: 1. Answers will vary; **2.** Answers will vary; **3.** C; **4.** B